M000119526

Dogspirations

SWEET & SIMPLE TRUTHS FROM OUR CANINE FRIENDS

Dogspirations

SWEET & SIMPLE TRUTHS FROM OUR CANINE FRIENDS

WILLOW CREEK PRESS®

Published by Willow Creek Press, Inc.
P.O. Box 147, Minocqua, Wisconsin 54548

Printed in China

Difficult roads lead to Beautiful destinations

When One Door Closes Another One Opens

Obstacles do not block the Path — they are the Path

IMAGINATION
Will Take
YOU EVERYWHERE

ALONE WE CAN DO SO LITTLE

Together

WE CAN DO SO MUCH

Failure is success in Progress

COLOR Outside THE Lines

LIFE IS

Better

WHEN YOU'RE

Laughing

DREAM
Bigger
THAN YOU CAN
Doubt

WHEN LIFE GETS

Blurry

ADJUST YOUR

Focus

Limits ARE FOR Those WHO NEED THEM

YOU CAN DO

Anything

BUT NOT EVERYTHING

FEAR IS
Temporary
REGRET IS
Forever

EVEN BAD

Chapters

CAN MAKE A STORY END WELL

IT'S THE
Will
NOT THE
Skill

IT TAKES A

Long Time

TO GROW AN OLD FRIEND

CREATIVE

Minds

ARE NEVER

Tidy

Bloom
WHERE YOU ARE
Planted

LIFE IS Short EAT DESSERT First

The struggle

IS ONLY PART OF THE

Story

Sometimes THE ONLY WAY OUT IS Through

BEING
Unique
IS BETTER THAN BEING
Perfect

ALL THINGS WORK

Together

FOR GOOD

Preparation is the key to Success

STORMS MAKE
Flowers
TAKE DEEPER ROOT

KEEP YOUR FACE TO THE

Sunshine

AND YOU CANNOT SEE THE SHADOWS

YOU ARE MORE

Capable

THAN YOU KNOW

TRY TO BE A

Rainbow

IN SOMEONE'S

Cloud

Embrace the Journey

SOME DAYS YOU JUST HAVE TO

Create

YOUR OWN SUNSHINE

Everything You Want Is On The Other Side Of Fear

ONE DAY OR Day One YOU DECIDE

IT TAKES

Strength

TO BE GENTLE AND KIND

DO NOT
Regret
THE PAST
Learn
FROM IT

Kindness COSTS Nothing

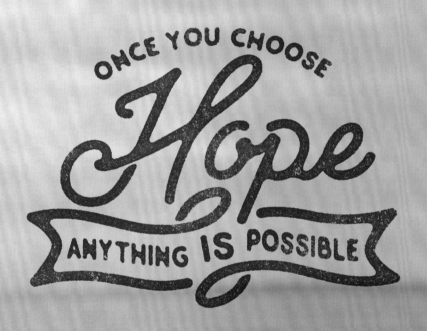